# ARISTOTLE IN 90 MINUTES

# Aristotle
## IN 90 MINUTES

Paul Strathern

IVAN R. DEE
CHICAGO

Library of Congress Cataloging-in-Publication Data:
Strathern, Paul, 1940–
    Aristotle in 90 minutes / Paul Strathern.
      p.   cm. — (Philosophers in 90 minutes)
    Includes bibliographical references and index.
    ISBN 1-56663-124-6 (cloth : alk. paper). —
    ISBN 1-56663-125-4 (paper : alk. paper)
    1. Aristotle.  I. Title.  II. Series.
B485.S783   1996
185—dc20                             96-24883

# Contents

# ARISTOTLE IN 90 MINUTES

# Introduction

Aristotle was perhaps the first and the greatest of all polymaths. He is known to have written on everything from the shape of seashells to sterility, from speculations on the nature of the soul to meteorology, poetry and art, and even the interpretation of dreams. He is said to have transformed every field of knowledge that he touched (apart from mathematics, where Plato and Platonic thought remained supreme). Above all, Aristotle is credited with the founding of logic.

When Aristotle first divided human knowledge into separate categories, this enabled our understanding of the world to develop in a systematic fashion. But in recent centuries our knowledge expanded to the point where it was being seriously hindered by this categorization. Such systems of thought allowed knowledge to develop only along certain predetermined paths, many of which were in danger of petering out. A radically different approach was needed. The result is the modern world of science.

The fact that it took us over twenty centuries to discover these limitations in Aristotle's thought only demonstrates his unparalleled originality. Yet even the demise of Aristotelian thought has given rise to many fascinating philosophical questions. How many more of these limitations have we yet to discover? How dangerous are these flaws in our way of thinking? And exactly what are they preventing us from learning?

# Aristotle's Life and Works

On a promontory above the village of Stagira, in northern Greece, stands a rather uninspired modern statue of Aristotle. Its expressionless face gazes out over the lumpy wooded hills toward the distant blue Aegean. Aristotle's pristine white marble form, almost luminescent in the brilliant sunlight, wears a décolleté toga and sandals, bearing a slightly chipped scroll in its left hand. (This damage is said to be the work of a souvenir-hunting Argentinean philosophy professor.) Carved into the plinth in Greek are the words "Aristotle the Stagirite."

Aristotle was born at Stagira, but despite the statue he wasn't born in the modern village of

Stagira. According to the guide book he was born in nearby ancient Stagira, whose ruins are still visible. After my disappointing encounter with the statue, I set off to find the ruins. These were somewhere just down the road, I was told by a young Batman returning home from school. With a flourish of his black plastic cloak, he indicated the road to the coast.

After an hour's sweltering walk down the long winding road, with the thunder rumbling ominously around the rocky hills above me, I was eventually given a lift to Stratoni, an eerie combination of deserted seaside resort and mining village. Ancient Stagira lay somewhere off the old road a bit farther to the north, I was told by a carpenter who was repairing the closed café on the empty waterfront.

Few cars travel on this road in October, as I was soon to discover. And the autumn storms in this region, when they eventually break, can be severe. For an hour I sheltered beneath a narrow ledge of rock as the torrential downpour cascaded over the bare hillside with no sign of ruins or vehicles visible in the flickering, crashing

10

gloom around me. Soaked to the skin, I raged to myself about the statue of Aristotle which had led me to Stagira, the wrong Stagira. It was nothing more than a fraud. The modern village of Stagira had no claim whatsoever to be known as Aristotle's birthplace, apart from fortuitously sharing the same name. Why, by the same token they might just as well erect a statue of Joan of Arc in New Orleans. . . .

Aristotle was born in 384 B.C. at ancient Stagira in Greek Macedonia. In the fourth century B.C. Macedonia was regarded by the ancient Greeks in much the same way as the modern French regard Britain and America. But Stagira was not beyond the pale of civilization. This was a small Greek colony founded by the Aegean island of Andros.

Aristotle's father Nicomachus had been personal physician to Amyntas, the king of Macedon and grandfather of Alexander the Great. As a result of this connection, which had ripened into friendship, Aristotle's father seems to have become a rich man, acquiring estates around Stagira and elsewhere in Greece. The young

Aristotle was brought up in an atmosphere of medical learning, but his father died when he was still young. Aristotle was then taken to Atarneus, a Greek city on the coast of Asia Minor, where he was brought up by his cousin Proxenus.

Like many an heir to a fortune, Aristotle soon began spending his inherited cash in determined fashion. According to one story, he blew the lot on wine, women, and song and ended up so broke that he was forced to join the army for a spell. After this he returned to Stagira where he took up medicine. Then, at the age of thirty, he gave it all up and set off for Athens to study at the Academy under Plato, where he remained for eight years. Later medieval hagiographers, determined to turn Aristotle into a saintly character, tended to ignore or discount these unthinkable calumnies. And sure enough, there is another version of Aristotle's early manhood. According to this rather more boring (but admittedly rather more credible) story, Aristotle went straight to the Academy at the age of seventeen. Yet even some of the sources for this story allude to a brief playboy interlude.

Either way, Aristotle soon settled down to a period of intense study at the Academy, quickly establishing himself as the finest mind of his generation. Initially he was a student, but he was soon invited to become one of Plato's colleagues. It seems that to begin with, Aristotle worshiped Plato. He certainly absorbed all the Platonic doctrine that was taught at the Academy, and his own philosophy was to be firmly grounded in its principles.

But Aristotle was far too bright to be a mere follower of anyone, even Plato. When Aristotle discerned what appeared to be a contradiction (or, heaven forbid, a flaw) in the works of his master, he felt it his intellectual duty to point this out. This habit soon began to irritate Plato, and though they appear not to have quarreled, the evidence suggests that the two greatest minds of their age soon found it politic to maintain a certain distance. Plato is known to have referred to Aristotle as "the mind on legs" and to have called his house "the reading shop." This latter remark referred to Aristotle's famous collection of ancient scrolls. Aristotle was in the habit of buying up as many rare scrolls of ancient works as he could lay his hands on, and was one of the first private citizens to own a library.

The young academic evidently received a considerable income from his inherited estates and soon became known in Athens for his cultured manners and gracious (if rather scholarly) lifestyle. Tradition has it that he was a weedy fellow, with spindly legs, who spoke with a lisp. Perhaps to compensate for this he became a natty dresser, donning the latest fashion in sandals and togas, and adorning his fingers with tastefully jeweled rings. Even Plato, who was no pauper, envied Aristotle his library. Yet despite Aristotle's comfortable and refined way of life, his early works (now lost) were mainly dialogues discussing the base futility of existence and the joys of the hereafter.

Aristotle had a natural inclination toward the practical and the scientific. This led him to view Plato's ideas from an increasingly realistic standpoint. Plato believed that the particular world we perceive around us consists of mere appearances. The ultimate reality lies in a further world of ideas, which resemble forms or ideals. The particular objects of the world we perceive derive their reality only by partaking in this ultimate world of ideas. Thus a particular cat, such as the black one I can see lying on the chair, is only a cat because it partakes in the ultimate idea (or form) of cattiness; and it is only black insofar as it partakes in the idea (or ideal) of black. The only true reality lies beyond the world we perceive—in this ultimate realm of ideas.

Where Plato's approach to the world was essentially religious, Aristotle's tended toward the scientific. This made him disinclined to dismiss the world around us as unreal. But he did continue to divide things into primary and secondary substances. Except that for Aristotle the primary substances were the particular objects of the world, and the secondary substances were the ideas or forms. Initially he dithered about which of these substances was in fact the ultimate reality, partly out of respect for Plato. (His old teacher had, after all, suggested this conception in the first place.) But gradually Aristotle became more and more convinced that he was living in the real world, and he shifted away from Plato's view.

Over the years Aristotle virtually turned Plato's philosophy on its head. Despite this, his metaphysical theories remain recognizably an adaptation of Plato's. Where Plato viewed forms as ideas that had a separate existence, Aristotle saw forms (or universals, as he called them) more as essences embodied in the substance of the world, with no separate existence of their own. Aristotle was to offer a number of devastating arguments against Plato's Theory of Ideas but appears not to have appreciated that these criticisms were equally devastating to his own Theory of Universals. Yet no one else seemed to notice this either. As a result, it was largely in the form of Aristotle's modified doctrine that Plato's theories were to become the dominant philosophy of the medieval world.

Fortunately there were many obscure points

and apparent contradictions in Aristotle's works, which gave medieval scholars food for endless controversy arising from different interpretations. These arguments over errors, heresies, schismatic misbeliefs, and devil-inspired misinterpretations kept alive the notion of philosophy, when to all intents and purposes the entire enterprise had died (or, perhaps more accurately, had entered a long Rip van Winkle period). It has been suggested that a number of these controversies arose from simple clerical errors, the result of medieval copyists inserting their own guesses in place of words that were no longer legible in the original worm-eaten texts.

In 347 B.C. Plato died, and the position of head of the Academy fell vacant. Half a dozen of Plato's most able colleagues judged there was only one man fit to take over this prestigious post. Unfortunately, each of them had a different man in mind (usually himself). Here Aristotle was no exception. To his disgust Speusippus, Plato's cousin, was eventually given the job. Speusippus is known to have been so bad-tempered that on one occasion he tossed his dog into a well for barking during his lectures. Eventually he administered euthanasia to himself after becoming an object of public ridicule during an exchange with Diogenes the Cynic in the Agora. Speusippus was scarcely the intellectual equal of the man whose doctrines were to lay the foundations for all serious intellectual thought for the next two millennia, and on his appointment Aristotle left Athens in high dudgeon, accompanied by his friend Xenocrates (another disappointed candidate).

Aristotle sailed across the Aegean to Atarneus, where he had spent his youth. This was now ruled by the eunuch Hermias, a Greek mercenary who had managed to take over this corner of Asia Minor. On a visit to Athens, Hermias had been highly impressed by what he had seen of the Academy, and he now welcomed Aristotle with open arms. Hermias was determined to make Atarneus a center of Greek culture, and Aristotle began advising him on the best way to go about this.

Aristotle's political philosophy consists largely of an examination of the different types of state, and how best they can be run. His understanding of politics is profound. This led him to adopt a pragmatic attitude, in direct contrast to Plato's idealistic approach. In *The Republic* Plato had described how a philosopher-king should rule his utopia (which, like any utopia, was in fact little more than a tyranny). Aristotle, on the other hand, described how to run an actual state, outlining effective courses of action that often almost anticipate Machiavelli.

Aristotle knew how politics worked and knew that it had to be effective to be of any use at all. This is not to say he was devoid of ideals. On the whole, Aristotle believed that the purpose of the state was to produce and support a class of cultured gentlemen such as himself— though he understands that this is not always possible. For instance, in order to run a tyranny successfully its ruler must behave like a tyrant. In such a police state there would be no room for Aristotle's cultured elite. Although at one point he does suggest that there is another way to run a tyranny: the tyrant can assume a religious pose and adopt a policy of moderation.

19

Some say this moderate approach is the one Aristotle probably adopted while tutoring the tyrant Hermias. In my view this is unlikely. Yet I am not suggesting that Aristotle would have advocated his own recommended means for maintaining a full-blown tyranny—which he described in chilling detail. In Aristotle's view, if you wished to run a tyranny properly it was necessary to run a tight ship. Liberal cultural activity must be banned and the population kept in fear and poverty and set to work building great public monuments, with occasional interludes of war to keep them alert and demonstrate their need to maintain a great leader. (Aristotle's analysis remains relevant, from Plato's philosopher-king to Saddam Hussein.)

Aristotle evolved his political philosophy during his later years. At the time he was tutoring Hermias he probably adhered to the ideas expressed in Plato's *Republic*. If so, he may well have tactfully modified Plato's doctrine of the philosopher-king. It was not necessary for a eunuch-tyrant to become a philosopher; instead

20

he should just be sure to follow the advice of one.

Aristotle was now approaching middle age. Despite his dandyism, he was considered very much the dry-as-dust professorial type. Then, to the surprise of all who knew him, Aristotle fell in love. The object of his affections was a young girl called Pythias, who is known to have been part of Hermias's household. Some say she was Hermias's sister, others that she was his adopted daughter. Other usually reliable sources claim that she was originally Hermias's concubine (which must have been something of a sinecure considering his sexual status). These contradictions suggest that she may well have been a palace courtesan. Was this an early case of the besotted professor falling for his Blue Angel?

Pythias wasn't a virgin when Aristotle married her, judging from his pronouncement: "once they have actually become married and call each other man and wife, it is quite wrong for a man or a woman to be unfaithful"—implying that before this it's okay. This pronouncement is found in Aristotle's remarks about adultery, and it appears that on such personal matters he was in the habit of generalizing from his own rather limited experience. In his remarks on marriage he asserts that the best age to marry is thirty-seven for a man and eighteen for a woman, precisely the ages at which he and Pythias were married. Brilliant though Aristotle may have been, imagination was not always his strong point.

This makes it all the more ironic that in his *Poetics* the prosaic Aristotle sets out the most influential elucidation of literature ever written while Plato, by far the most poetically gifted of all the philosophers, decreed that poets should be banned. (What was Plato trying to hide, one wonders.) Aristotle had a high regard for poetry, claiming that it was of more value than history because it was more philosophical. History deals only with particular events, whereas poetry is closer to the universal. Here he appears to be contradicting himself and echoing Plato's worldview. But Aristotle's celebrated assertion that tragedy "arouses pity and fear so that such emotions are purged by the performance" remains a cardinal insight into the moving but problematic experience of tragic drama.

Being a profound and essentially serious character, Aristotle found himself out of his depth when it came to comedy. In his opinion, comedy is the imitation of inferior people, and ludicrousness is merely a painless form of ugliness. Aesthetics can only attempt to clear up the mess created by art, and theoreticians of comedy usually end up on a banana peel. Aristotle is no exception, observing that "To begin with, comedy was not taken seriously."

Not long after his marriage Aristotle founded a school at Assos. Three years later he moved on to Mytilene, on the island of Lesbos, where he founded another school. By this time Aristotle is known to have been deeply interested in the classification of plants and animals. One of his favorite haunts for specimen hunting was the shores of the all but landlocked Yera Gulf, whose still blue waters beneath Mount Olympus are as idyllic today as they must have been then. In spring the slopes are covered by a multicolored carpet of flowers, and in Aristotle's day there would have been wolves, wild boar, lynx, and even bear in the mountains: the first naturalist's paradise for the first naturalist. In his works on nature Aristotle attempted to discover a hierarchy of classes and species but was overwhelmed by the sheer volume of his research. He was convinced that nature had a purpose and that each feature of an animal was there for a function. "Nature does nothing in vain," he claimed. It was to be well over two millennia before biology made any effective advance on this notion, with Darwin's theory of evolution.

By now Aristotle had acquired a reputation as the leading intellectual throughout Greece. Philip of Macedon had recently overrun Greece, for the first time uniting its bickering city-states into one sovereign country, and he invited Aristotle to become tutor to his unruly young son Alexander. As Aristotle's father had been personal physician and friend to Philip's father, Aristotle was considered one of the family, and he felt obliged to accept this regal offer. Reluctantly he set out for the Macedonian capital of Pella.

Nowadays Pella is little more than a field of stones, with some pebble mosaics and half a dozen columns, beside the busy main road from Thessaloniki to the western Greek border. It is a surprisingly unimpressive spot, considering that this was the first capital of ancient Greece; and later, after Alexander the Great launched his campaign to conquer the world, it could even have claimed to be the first (and last) capital of the known world.

Here in 343 B.C. one of the finest minds the world has ever known set about trying to educate one of the greatest megalomaniacs the world has ever known. Aristotle was forty-two years old, Alexander was thirteen, but not surprisingly it was Alexander who won hands down. The headstrong young pupil learned absolutely nothing from his tutor during the three years of their association. Or so the story goes. Aristotle was convinced of the superiority of the Greeks to all other races. In his eyes the finest leader would be a Homeric hero, such as Achilles, whose mind had been exposed to the latest advances in Greek civilization; and he believed that in man's mind lay an ability to subdue the entire world. There's no denying that Alexander bore an uncanny resemblance to this blueprint, even if he did not turn out quite as Aristotle might have wished. But we can only speculate on this meeting of minds, about which curiously little is known.

What is known is that in payment for his services Aristotle asked Philip to rebuild his birthplace, Stagira, which had inadvertently been reduced to rubble during one of Philip's recent campaigns in the Halkidiki peninsula. And there is evidence that while Alexander was on his great expedition of conquest, he sent back assorted unknown plants and a zoo of exotic animals for his old tutor to classify. Horticultural lore has it that this was how the first rhododendrons reached Europe from central Asia. If so, Aristotle must have misclassified this species: rhododendron means rose tree in ancient Greek.

In 336 B.C. Philip of Macedon was assassinated, and the sixteen-year-old Alexander assumed the throne. After speedily executing all other possible claimants, and embarking on a few preliminary blitzkrieg campaigns through Macedonia, Albania, up through Bulgaria and across the Danube, and down through Greece (reducing Thebes to a smoking ruin en route), Alexander set off on his campaign to conquer the known world. In practice this included North Africa, and Asia as far as Tashkent and northern India. Fortunately Aristotle's geography lessons hadn't mentioned China, whose existence was unknown to the West at this time.

Meanwhile Aristotle had returned to Stagira. But before he had left Pella, Aristotle had recommended his cousin Calisthenes to Alexander for the position of court intellectual. This act of generosity was to prove all but fatal for Aristotle. Calisthenes was a bit of a blabbermouth, and Aristotle warned him about talking too much at court before he left. When Alexander set out on his world-beating campaign, he took along Calisthenes as his official historian. But while they were fighting their way through Persia, Calisthenes appears to have talked himself into a charge of treason. Whereupon Alexander had him locked up in a portable cage. As Calisthenes trailed alongside the army in his cage, languishing in the desert heat, his body became covered with sores and crawling insects, until in the end Alexander became so sick of the sight of him that he threw him to a lion. But like all successful megalomaniacs Alexander had his paranoid streak: he blamed Aristotle for Calisthenes' treachery. Alexander is said to have been on the point of signing orders for Aristotle's death, but in the end he set off to conquer India instead.

After spending five years in Stagira, Aristotle returned to Athens. Then in 335 B.C. Speusippus died, and the position of head of the Academy once again fell vacant. This time it was given to Aristotle's old friend Xenocrates, who was considered a suitably austere and dignified character despite having once been awarded a gold crown "for his prowess in drinking at the Feast of Pitchers." (Xenocrates was to die in office twenty years later by tripping in the night and falling into a cistern.)

Aristotle was so miffed at being passed over once again that he decided to found a rival school of his own. This he established in a large gymnasium beyond the city walls beneath Mount Lycabettos. The gymnasium was attached to the nearby Temple of Apollo Lyceus (Apollo in the form of a wolf). Thus Aristotle's school became known as the Lyceum. The name lives on to this day, most appropriately in the French word *lycée*, though precisely why Aristotle's great school should also be commemorated in the names of ballrooms and theaters is not so clear. Aristotle's original Lyceum certainly taught a wide range of subjects, but ballroom dancing and acting were not to achieve full-fledged academic status until the twentieth century in the American Midwest.

The Lyceum was much more like a modern university than the Academy. A new leader was elected to the student council every ten days, separate faculties competed for students, and occasional attempts were even made to institute a schedule of classes. The Lyceum undertook research in the different sciences, passing on its findings to the students; the Academy was more interested in giving its students sufficient grounding in politics and law, so that they could become future rulers of the city. The Lyceum was the MIT (or even the Institute of Advanced Studies) of its day, whereas the Academy more resembled nineteenth-century Oxford or the Sorbonne.

The differences between the Lyceum and the Academy aptly illustrate the differences between the philosophies of Aristotle and Plato. Where Plato wrote *The Republic*, Aristotle preferred to collect copies of the constitutions of all the Greek city-states and select the best points from each. The Lyceum was the school that city-states turned to when they wished to have a new constitution written. No one tried to set up the Republic. Unfortunately Aristotle's exhaustive study of politics had already been rendered practically redundant—by none other than his worst pupil, Alexander. The face of the world was changing forever: Alexander's new empire was bringing about the end of the city-state, much as today continental confederations may well bring about the effective end of the independent nation-state. Neither Aristotle nor any of the galaxy of intellectuals gathered in the schools of Athens appear to have noticed this great historical change, an omission on a par with nineteenth-century intellectuals from Marx to Nietzsche failing to foresee the supremacy of the United States.

Aristotle gave his lectures at the Lyceum while walking with his pupils, and hence his school of followers became known as the Peripatetics (those who walk up and down). Some, however, claim they received this name because their master gave his lectures in the sheltered arcade of the gymnasium (known as the Peripatos).

Aristotle is credited with the founding of logic (it was over two thousand years before a logician of similar caliber was to appear); he was a metaphysician almost on a par with Plato; and he surpassed his master in both ethics and epistemology. (Despite this, Plato has the edge on him as an originator. Aristotle may have come up with the answers, but Plato was the one to see the basic questions which we should be asking in the first place.)

Aristotle's most significant achievement was in the field of logic. To all intents he invented this subject. Aristotle came to see logic as the foundation on which all learning is based. Plato had understood that knowledge could be discovered by dialectic (conversational argument by means of question and answer), but it was Aristotle who formalized and advanced this method with his discovery of the syllogism. According to Aristotle, the syllogism showed that "when certain things are stated, it can be shown that something other than what is stated necessarily follows." For example, if we make the following two statements:

All humans are mortal.

All Greeks are human.

It can be inferred that:

All Greeks are mortal.

This is logically necessary and undeniable. Aristotle distinguished between different types of syllogism, involving negatives or limited cases, but they all had the same basic structure. The major premise is followed by a minor premise, which leads to a conclusion. Thus:

No philosophers are dunces.

Some humans are philosophers.

Therefore some humans are not dunces.

To our present way of thinking, this type of argument appears hopelessly cumbersome and liable to lead to all kinds of woolly thought. But in its day it represented a categorical advance in human thinking—of a magnitude that has remained unsurpassed before or since. That is not to say it doesn't have certain definite flaws. For instance, the syllogism:

All horses are animals.

All horses have hooves.

Therefore some animals have hooves.

This argument is valid only if there are such things as horses. As is shown by the following syllogism of the same structure:

All unicorns are horses.

All unicorns have horns.

Therefore some horses have horns.

Aristotle called his logic "analytika," which means unraveling. Every science or field of knowledge had to start from a set of first principles, or axioms. From these its truths could be deduced by logic (or unraveled). These axioms defined the subject's field of activity, separating it from irrelevant or incompatible elements. Biology and poetry, for instance, started from mutually exclusive premises. Thus mythical beasts were not a part of biology, and biology had no need to be written in the form of poetry. This logical approach released entire fields of knowledge, giving them the potential to discover whole new sets of truths. It was to be two millennia before these definitions became a stranglehold, restricting the development of human knowledge.

Aristotle's thinking *was* philosophy through many centuries to come, and in the Middle Ages it came to be regarded as gospel, preventing further development. Aristotle's thinking may have built the intellectual edifice of the medieval world, but it was hardly his fault that this eventually became a prison.

Aristotle himself would never have allowed

this. His works are littered with the kinds of inconsistencies that show a continually questioning and developing mind. He preferred research into the actual workings of the world to mere speculation about its nature. Even his mistakes often appear to have a poetic insight—"anger is the boiling of blood around the heart," "the eye is made blue by the sky." In true Greek fashion he saw education as the way forward for humanity, believing that an educated man differed from an uneducated one "as much as the living from the dead." Yet his understanding of the place of education was not that of a shallow optimist: "it is an ornament in prosperity, and a refuge in adversity." He may have ended a bit of a pedant, but he gives indication of having known his share of suffering. He remained a teacher throughout his life and never sought to hold public office, yet no man throughout human history has ever had such a lasting effect on the world.

In this we are fortunate, for Aristotle seems to have been a good man. He saw the goal of humanity as the pursuit of happiness, which he defined as the actualization of the best we are capable of. But what *is* the best we are capable of? In Aristotle's view, reason is man's highest faculty. Therefore "the best (and happiest) man spends as much of his time as possible in the purest activity of reason, which is theorizing." This is very much an innocent professorial view of happiness: hedonism as a purely theoretical pursuit. Few in the real world would subscribe to such a view (and those who do don't seem to be any happier than the thoughtless philistine enjoying his lottery winnings).

Similar objections apply to Aristotle's view that we should try to actualize what we do best. It is arguable that his famous pupil Alexander sought the actualization of the best he was capable of—inflicting suffering and death on countless thousands in the process. Yet it can also be argued that Aristotle sought to check such moral excesses with his famous doctrine of the Golden Mean.

According to this idea, every virtue is the mean between two extremes. This recalls the traditional Greek concept of moderation, mentioned even in the works of Homer, who pre-dated Aristotle by some five hundred years and described events that had taken place a millen-nium before the philosopher's birth. The early Greeks (and indeed the later ancient Greeks) were in great need of a concept of moderation. "Nothing too much" was soon adopted as one of their chief maxims of moral guidance. Such was their abundant energy that when it was not channeled into creative endeavors it frequently found outlet in excess. The frenzied and orgiastic behavior associated with the worshipers of Dionysius; the dark aspects of character and rit-ual that persisted into Greek tragedy; the terrors and superstitions of everyday life—these are the shadow side of the early classical era. For philos-ophy, mathematics, and artistic excellence to emerge from such chaos, supreme moderation was required.

Characteristically Pythagoras even tried to ally this moderation to mathematics, so that the virtue between two extremes could be calcu-lated. Everything without measure, or unmeasurable (such as infinity), was evil. Exactitude became a virtue. (Strong elements of this remain recognizable in Western morality to this day.)

Plato, with his love of the mathematical and the abstract, appears to go along with much of this. Aristotle, on the other hand, was against the mathematical approach to morals. It was not possible to calculate what is good. The good was not to be determined by purely abstract considerations; it was more akin to the harmony found in a work of art. Moral virtue was a mean between two extremes, but this depended more upon a person's nature and the situation in which he found himself. To kill a man on the battlefield was different from killing one on the street; and even here, if you killed him in the furtherance of a robbery it was different from doing so if he had grievously wronged you. Along with Aristotle's view of harmony came a necessary element of relativism. And this too exhibited moderation.

The difficulty arises when you attempt to formulate this morality in any detail. If, according to the Golden Mean, every virtue lies between two extremes, what precisely are these extremes? Without ancient Greek fervor, and intimacy with dangerous extremes, such a doctrine leads only to mediocrity or verbal juggling. To call telling the truth halfway between telling a lie and correcting a falsehood is ingenious but ethically vacuous. (Aristotle didn't maintain this but would have needed to come up with something like it to fill the gap in his argument.)

During Aristotle's later years his wife Pythias died. Marriage obviously suited him, for he now married his maidservant Herpyllis, who was to be the mother of his first son Nicomachus. In 323 B.C. news reached Athens that Alexander had died in Babylon, at the end of a prolonged drinking bout with his generals. The Athenians had long resented being under the domination of the uncultured Macedonians, and at Alexander's death they gave vent to their feelings. Aristotle, who had been born in Macedonia and was renowned for having tutored its ablest son, became a victim of this wave of anti-Macedonian feeling. He was arraigned on a trumped-up charge of impiety, his accuser Eurymedon the hierophant citing the eulogy he had written twenty years earlier on the death of his benefactor, the eunuch Hermias of Atarneus. This had contained the lines:

"Sons of the gods strove for thee
And the Heroes returned to the earth
All for thy love and thee to see."

This was hardly impiety, but the mob required victims. If Aristotle had stood trial he would certainly have been sentenced to death. But Aristotle was not made of the same stuff as Socrates; he had no inclination toward martyrdom. Wisely he fled the city to prevent Athens from "sinning twice against philosophy."

This was no easy decision. It involved Aristotle abandoning his beloved Lyceum forever. Deprived of his library and access to his research archives, the aging philosopher now retired to property in Chalkis which he had inherited from his father. This city lies thirty miles north of Athens on the long island of Euboea, at the point where it is separated from the mainland by a narrow channel. The waters of this channel are subject to an unexplained phenomenon. Despite the Aegean being virtually tideless, a rapid current runs through the channel, changing directions for no accountable reason as many as a dozen times a day. A persistent local myth has it that Aristotle spent many days racking his brains for an explanation of this phenomenon and when, for the first time in his life he found himself defeated, he jumped into the water and drowned.

More reliable historical sources record that Aristotle died in 322 B.C. at the age of sixty-three, a year after arriving in Chalkis. He is said to have died of a stomach illness, though one source claims he committed suicide by drinking aconite, a poisonous extract made from wolfsbane. In those days this was sometimes used as a medicament, which suggests to me an accidental overdose or self-administered euthanasia rather than straight suicide. But it's possible that his bitter disappointment at losing the Lyceum brought him to the point where he no longer considered life worth living.

Aristotle's will begins with the immortal words: "All will be well, but in case anything should happen . . ." It goes on to outline instructions for the care of his children and the granting of freedom to his slaves. He then informs his executor that if Herpyllis wishes to marry again, "she should be given to someone not unworthy." The author of this document comes through as an essentially prosaic, decent man, his character utterly unwarped by being the vehicle of supreme genius. He ends his will by requesting that part of the money he leaves be used to erect life-sized statues of Zeus and Athena in Stagira.

I detected no sign of these statues when I finally arrived at the scattered, rain-swept stones of ancient Stagira during the tail end of a thunderstorm on that unfortunate afternoon several years ago in Greece. As I blundered about over the godforsaken hillside, I found myself reminded of Aristotle's insight into the nature of comedy. According to him, the ludicrous was merely a form of painless ugliness. Numb with cold, and not a pretty sight, I realized there was still some mileage left in Aristotle's thought, at least where the ludicrous was concerned.

Aristotle's originality remains unparalleled in

the history of philosophy. Despite this, he suffered from the oldest philosophical delusion of them all, one that remains with us to this day. According to Cicero: "Aristotle criticized the philosophers who preceded him for thinking that their intellectual effort had been sufficient to complete philosophy once and for all. He was convinced they must have been either very stupid or very conceited to think such a thing. However, as philosophy had made such great strides in just a few years, he was confident that it would soon be brought to a successful conclusion."

# Afterword

When Aristotle was forced to flee Athens in 323 B.C., he left the Lyceum in charge of Theophrastus. According to one source, Theophrastus had fallen in love with Aristotle's son, who had been his pupil, but Aristotle evidently didn't consider that this time-honored occupational hazard disqualified his successor. Theophrastus ensured the continuity of the Lyceum after the departure of its founder, and its Peripatetic School of philosophers soon began living up to their name by wandering throughout the classical world, spreading Aristotelian philosophy wherever they went.

Yet it was some three centuries after the

45

death of Aristotle before his works were gathered in the form we know them today. Aristotle's works can be divided into two groups—those he wrote for publication, and his lecture notes at the Lyceum (which were not intended for publication). Inevitably all the former have been lost, and the only works of Aristotle that have come down to us are the latter. These were originally in fragmented form and covered hundreds of scrolls. They were organized into various distinct works by Andronicus of Rhodes, who was the last head of the Lyceum. It is to Andronicus that we owe the word *metaphysics*—the title he gave to a group of Aristotle's works. These originally had no title and merely followed those on physics, thus Andronicus simply labeled them "after physics," which in ancient Greek is "metaphysics." The works in this section consisted of Aristotle's treatises on ontology (the nature and relations of being) and the ultimate nature of things. This subject quickly became identified with the label that had been attached to these works: metaphysics. So this word, which through the centuries has become synonymous with philosophy itself, originally had nothing to do with the philosophy it described. Just like philosophy itself, it began with a mistake and has continued to flourish as such ever since.

During the classical era Aristotle was not regarded as one of the great Greek philosophers (on a par with the likes of Socrates or Plato). In Roman times Aristotle was acknowledged as the great logician, but his other philosophy was largely eclipsed by (or absorbed into) the evolving Neoplatonism. And over the centuries this was in turn largely absorbed into Christianity.

Christian thinkers quickly recognized the usefulness of Aristotle's logic; thus Aristotle now came into his own as the supreme authority for philosophical method. Aristotelian logic was to remain the basis of sound theological debate throughout the Middle Ages. Ambitious monastic intellectuals indulged in nit-picking logical argument, the finest minds using this expertise to hunt out heresies. Aristotle's theologically unobjectionable logic thus became an integral part of the Christian canon.

Yet parallel to this European Christian development of Aristotle's thought was another, equally important, Eastern development, which was eventually to have a profound effect on medieval Europe.

During the early centuries of the first millennium A.D., the body of Aristotle's work remained lost to the Western world. Only in the Middle East did scholars continue to study the full range of his philosophy. The seventh century saw the rise of Islam followed by widespread Arabic conquest throughout the Middle East. Islamic intellectuals quickly recognized the merits of Aristotle's works, discerning in them no conflict with their religious faith, and began interpreting them for their own purposes. Aristotle's teachings were soon absorbed to the point where almost all Islamic philosophy was derived from interpretations of his thought. It was the Arabs who first understood that Aristotle was one of the great philosophers. While the Western world sank into the Dark Ages, the Islamic world continued to develop intellectually. Indicative of this rich heritage are the words we have absorbed from Arabic, such as *algebra*, *alcohol*, and *al-*

*chemy*. But greatest of all was their use of Arabic numerals while in the Western world mathematics remained hamstrung by the use of Roman numerals. Divide LXXXVII by XLIV, using only Roman numerals, and the difficulties of more refined calculation immediately become apparent. Not for nothing is it said that the only Roman who appears in the history of mathematics is the soldier who slew Archimedes.

In the East, Aristotelian philosophy was developed by two great Islamic scholars. Abu Aki Al-Husayn Ibn Abd Allah Ibn Sana (fortunately known to us as Avicenna) was born in Persia at the end of tenth century and emerged as one of the greatest philosopher-scientists of the Islamic world. His voluminous works on medicine were among the finest ever written, noble attempts to lift this subject from the quackery that it has never quite been able to forswear. Avicenna even attempted to remedy what he saw as elements of quackery in the works of Aristotle. He discerned various problems that Aristotle had overlooked, and even gave answers to these problems such as Aristotle might have given had he seen them in the first place. His attempts to render Aristotle's thought more systematic are masterly and tie up many loose ends. Unfortunately much of Avicenna's work only closed off options that Aristotle had always wished to be left open. Aristotle knew he couldn't know everything—Avicenna felt otherwise.

The other great Islamic commentator on Aristotle was Averroës, who lived in twelfth-century Moorish Spain and became personal physician *cum* philosopher to the caliphs of Cordoba. Averroës was convinced that philosophy, and in particular the philosophy of Aristotle, was the real way to the truth, that revelations of belief were merely a lower form of arriving at God. Reason was far superior to faith. (It would be more than five hundred years before such heretical thoughts began to surface in Christian Europe.)

One day the caliph disturbed Averroës by asking him how the heavens had come into existence. The philosopher was forced to confess that he had no answer to this question (not always a healthy intellectual position to adopt with a caliph who employs you to answer his questions). Fortunately the caliph respected Averroës's honesty and sent him away to find the answer in Aristotle.

For the next thirty years Averroës wrote an endless stream of commentaries and interpretations on Aristotle's work. Wisely he never came up with an answer to the caliph's original question: the caliph himself had already pronounced on this matter. But Averroës did advance several of his own answers to Aristotle, even providing arguments from Aristotle to support his point of view (which often contradicted Aristotle's).

This was just the kind of approach that appealed to medieval Christian scholars, who quickly perceived its uses in the persecution of heretics. Translations of Averroës's commentaries on Aristotle began circulating in Paris, the great center of learning at the time. But the Averroists, as they became known, soon found themselves in trouble. Aristotle may have been accepted by the church, but these new teachings of his looked suspiciously unorthodox. In the conflict between reason and faith, there could be no doubting the supremacy of faith. The Averroists found themselves facing the prospect of a heresy charge, and the only way they could defend themselves was to use arguments from the same source as their heresy—namely, the writings of Averroës.

Fortunately the situation was remedied by Thomas Aquinas, the greatest of the medieval scholars, who managed to patch up a compromise. Reason must indeed be free to operate according to its own inexorable laws, suggested Aquinas, but only from within the confines of faith. Reason without faith was nothing.

Aquinas was deeply attracted to Aristotle and quickly recognized his supreme worth. He devoted much of his life to reconciling Aristotle's philosophy with that of the church. In the end he succeeded in establishing Aristotelianism as the philosophical basis for Christian theology. This was to be the making, and eventual breaking, of Aristotelianism. The Catholic church pronounced that the teachings of Aristotle—as interpreted by Aquinas—were The Truth and could be denied only on pain of heresy (a situation which remains in force to this day). Much of Aristotle's philosophy concerned the natural world and was thus scientific. Science, like philosophy, makes pronouncements that appear to be the truth but later turn out to be wrong. They must be modified as our understanding of the world increases. By declaring the works of Aristotle to be the holy writ, the church painted itself into a corner (and the corner of a flat earth, at that). Conflict between the church and scientific discovery was thus inevitable. Aristotle is not responsible for this conflict between reason and faith, which was not satisfactorily resolved in Western thought until this century. Indeed, like Count Dracula it still makes the odd sensational resurrection when night returns to the world of learning. The argument raging in some of the United States between Darwinism (evolution) and creationism (the literal truth of the Bible) is but a recent example.

Despite the demise of Aristotelian thought, Aristotle himself has continued to play a part in modern philosophy. The contemporary American philosopher of science Thomas Kuhn, a profound admirer of Aristotle, found himself puzzled that such a supreme genius could also be guilty of making a number of simple errors. For instance, despite some earlier philosophers realizing that the earth orbited the sun, Aristotle remained convinced that the earth was the center of the universe—an error which severely restricted astronomical knowledge for more than fifteen hundred years. Scientific thought was likewise hindered by Aristotle's belief that the world was made up of four primary elements: earth, air, fire, and water. Kuhn's study of Aristotle's errors led him to formulate his notion of paradigms, which revolutionized our thinking about the philosophy of science and had applications far beyond this field.

According to Kuhn, Aristotle was led into error because of the *way* he and his contemporaries viewed the world: the paradigm of their thought. The ancient Greeks saw the world as consisting essentially of qualities—shape, purpose, and so forth. Viewing the world in this way, they were *bound* to arrive at a number of wrongheaded conclusions, such as those which marred even Aristotle's thought.

The inevitable conclusion to be drawn from Kuhn's notion of paradigms is that there can be no such thing as a "true" way of viewing the world, either scientifically or philosophically. The conclusions we reach simply depend upon the paradigms we adopt: the way we decide to think about the world. In other words, there is no such thing as ultimate truth.

# From Aristotle's Writings

We make war so that we can live in peace.
   —*Nicomachean Ethics*, Book 10, 1177b 5–6

## THE OBJECT OF LIFE

All our arts and enquiries, just the same as all our actions and choices, are thought of as trying to achieve some good. For this reason, we can correctly define the Good as "that which all things aim at." Yet obviously there is a difference between the ends at which things aim. Some of these ends are activities, whereas some are results distinct from activities. Where the ends are distinct from the actions, the results are naturally superior to the activities. Because there are all kinds of arts, activities, and sciences, it is inevitable that they have all kinds of different ends as well. The end of medical science is health; the end of military science is victory; the end of economic science is wealth.

—*Nicomachean Ethics*, Book 1, 1094a 1

Human good turns out to be the active exercise of the soul in conformity with excellence or virtue, and if there is more than one excellence or virtue, in conformity with the best and most complete. But this activity must take place throughout a complete lifetime, for one swallow does not make a summer, any more than one fine day. Likewise, one day or a brief flight of happiness does not make a man completely blessed or happy.

—*Nicomachean Ethics*, Book 1, 1098a 16–19

Tragedy is the representation of an action that is worthy of serious attention, involves greatness, will subscribe, must therefore be taken from the definition of right which is common to both.

—*Politics*, 1318a 19–28

The objects of mathematics are not substances in any higher sense than things. They are only logically prior, not prior in being, to sensible things. Mathematical entities can in no way exist on their own. But since they cannot exist in perceivable objects either, they must therefore not exist at all, or exist in some special way which does not imply independent existence. For "to exist" can mean many different things.

—*Metaphysics*, 1077b 12–17

Where natural bodies are concerned, some have life and some do not. That is to say, some are able to nourish themselves, to grow and to decay. Thus every living natural body, which must be substance, must also be a complex substance. But since it is a body of a particular kind—that is to say, it has life—the body cannot

and takes place over an extended time yet is complete within itself ... portraying incidents which arouse pity and fear, so that such emotions are purged by the performance.

—*Poetics*, 1449b 24–28

He who studies how things originated and came into being, whether this is the state or anything else, will achieve the clearest view of them.

—*Politics*, 1252a 24–25

Thus it is clear that the state is a creation of nature. . . . And it is one of man's characteristics that he alone possesses a sense of good and evil, justice and injustice, and such, and the coming together of living beings who possess this sense makes a family and a state.

—*Politics*, 1253a 2–18

The notion of the state is naturally prior to that of the family or the individual, for the whole must necessarily be prior to the parts. If you re-move the whole man, you can't say a foot or a hand remains, unless you look upon this as if it were made of stone—for it would only be dead. A thing is only understood to be what it is owing to its abilities and its power to perform them. And when it no longer has these abilities or power, it no longer remains the same thing, it merely has the same name. It is thus obvious that a city precedes an individual. For if an individual isn't sufficient in himself to form a perfect gov-ernment, he is simply to a city what other parts are to a whole. And anyone who is unable to live in society, or doesn't need to because he is suffi-cient unto himself, must be either a beast or a god. Thus everyone has a natural impulse to as-sociate with others in this way, and whoever founded the first civil society brought about the greatest good to humanity. In this way man is the finest of all living creatures, just as without laws and justice he would be the worst. For nothing is so difficult to eradicate as injustice perpetrated by force. But man is born with this force—which is both prudence and valor—and

it can be used for both just and unj poses. Those who abuse this force wil most iniquitous, lustful, and gluttonous imaginable. On the other hand, justice binds men to the state; for the adminis of justice, which consists of determining just, is the principle of order in political sc
—*Politics*, 1253a

Democrats maintain that democracy is wh majority decide; those who favor oligarchi lieve that those with the most wealth shoul cide. But both these ways are unjust. If we fe what is proposed by the few, we soon ha tyranny. For if one person possesses more any others, according to oligarchical justice man alone has the right to supreme power. the other hand, if superiority of numbers is criteria that prevails, injustice will be perpetra by the confiscation of the property of the ri who will be in the minority and thus have say. The notion of equality, to which both parti

be soul. For a body is a subject, not something predicated to a subject, and is thus matter. The soul is therefore substance in the sense that it is the form of a natural body, which potentially has life. Substance in this sense is actuality. In this way the soul is the actuality of the living body. But actuality has two senses, which are similar to the possession of knowledge and the use of knowledge. The actuality of which we are speaking is similar to the possession of knowledge. For both sleeping and waking require the presence of a soul—and waking is like the use of knowledge, whereas sleeping is similar to the possession of knowledge without using it.

—*De Anima*, 412a 17–26

It is obvious that there are causes, and many of them. These are discovered when we begin asking: "Why did this happen?" This leads us back to several basic questions. When faced with unchangeable things, we are left asking: "What is it?" For example, in mathematics it all comes down to the definition of a straight line or number or some such. Or in other cases we might be led to ask: "What brought about this change?" As for instance in: "Why did these people go to war?" The answer here could be: "Because of border raids." Or it could be because what the thing itself is for: in other words, they fought for dominion. In another category, where things come to be, their cause will be matter.

Evidently these are the causes. There are several different types of causes, and anyone who wishes to understand nature should know how to uncover them. In fact, there are four different types: matter, form, whatever brings about the change, and whatever the thing is for.

—*Physics*, 198a 14–24

Thus motion, being eternal, if there is a prime mover it too must be eternal ... and here it is sufficient to assume there is only one mover, the first to set in motion stationary things, and this being eternal will be the principle of motion for all other things.

—*Physics*, 259a 7–14

64

*Aristotle wrote and thought so originally about so many things that he was bound to get a few of them wrong:*

People whose nostrils have thick extremities are lazy, just like cattle. Those who have thick ends to their noses are insensitive, just like boars. On the other hand, people who have sharp-ended noses are easily angered, much like dogs. However, those with round flat ends to their noses are magnanimous, in the same way as lions. People with thin tips to their noses are like birds; but when their nose is hooked and juts out straight from their forehead they are liable to shameless behavior (just like ravens).

—*Physiognomics*, VI 28–36

*Aristotle did much to establish scientific investigation and categorization. His achievements are astonishing, especially when one considers much of the current evidence and material in this field, some of which he recorded:*

In Arabia there is said to be a species of hyena which paralyzes its prey by its mere presence. If this hyena steps into the shadow of a man, it not only paralyzes him but renders him completely dumb. . . . There are two rivers in Euboea. The cattle that drink from the one called Cerbes turn white, and those that drink from the one called Neleus turn black. . . . The river Rhenus flows in the opposite direction to other rivers, running to the north where the Germans live. In the summer its waters are navigable, but in the winter it is frozen with ice, so that the people can walk on it like land.

—*On Marvelous Things Heard*, 145, 168

*For centuries many of Aristotle's contributions to philosophy were considered sacrosanct. His truths were "eternal truths" which could never be denied. But the advent of modern philosophy led to the gradual discarding of Aristotelian thought. Surely his most important contribution, logic, would last forever. Then came Nietzsche, and even this was called into question:*

We cannot both affirm and deny the same thing. This is a subjective empirical law—nothing to do with logical "necessity," only of our inability to do it.

In Aristotle's view the law of contradiction is the most certain basic principle of them all. It is the ultimate and most fundamental principle upon which all demonstrative proof rests. The principles of every axiom depend upon it. Yet if this is really the case we should perhaps examine more thoroughly what *presuppositions* are already involved here. Either it says something about actuality, about being, as if we already knew it from another source; that is, as if opposite attributes *could* not be ascribed to it. Or it means: opposite attributes *should* not be ascribed to it. In which case, logic would not be an imperative to know the truth, as formerly supposed, but merely an imperative to organize a world that we could look upon as the true one.

Thus it remains an open question—Do the axioms of logic precisely match reality? Or are they simply a means and method for us to *create* a concept of "reality" that suits us? As already indicated, to agree with the first question we would have to possess a previous knowledge of being (i.e., one prior to our use of, and in no way involved with, logic). And this is certainly not the case. The proposition (the one that forms the law of contradiction) thus involves no criteria of truth. It is simply an *imperative* saying what *should* count as true.

—Nietzsche, *Will to Power*, Sec 516

*Logic thus becomes the morality of our way of viewing and perceiving the world—the ethics of our epistemology. To deny it is "wrong," not in a factual sense but in a moral sense. Our entire notion of truth—logical, scientific, religious, the need to tell it socially, and so forth—are thus in the same category. They are systems by which we live, which are of use and benefit to us. They are not based upon what actually happens but upon what is useful to us and fits in with how we choose to view the world.*

# Chronology of Significant
# Philosophical Dates

| | |
|---|---|
| 6th C B.C. | The beginning of Western philosophy with Thales of Miletus. |
| End of 6th C B.C. | Death of Pythagoras. |
| 399 B.C. | Socrates sentenced to death in Athens. |
| c 387 B.C. | Plato founds the Academy in Athens, the first university. |
| 335 B.C. | Aristotle founds the Lyceum in Athens, a rival school to the Academy. |

| | |
|---|---|
| 324 A.D. | Emperor Constantine moves capital of Roman Empire to Byzantium. |
| 400 A.D. | St. Augustine writes his *Confessions*. Philosophy absorbed into Christian theology. |
| 410 A.D. | Sack of Rome by Visigoths heralds opening of Dark Ages. |
| 529 A.D. | Closure of Academy in Athens by Emperor Justinian marks end of Hellenic thought. |
| Mid-13th C | Thomas Aquinas writes his commentaries on Aristotle. Era of Scholasticism. |
| 1453 | Fall of Byzantium to Turks, end of Byzantine Empire. |
| 1492 | Columbus reaches America. Renaissance in Florence and revival of interest in Greek learning. |
| 1543 | Copernicus publishes *On the Revolution of the Celestial Orbs*, proving mathematically that the earth revolves around the sun. |

| 1633 | Galileo forced by church to recant heliocentric theory of the universe. |
| 1641 | Descartes publishes his *Meditations*, the start of modern philosophy. |
| 1677 | Death of Spinoza allows publication of his *Ethics*. |
| 1687 | Newton publishes *Principia*, introducing concept of gravity. |
| 1689 | Locke publishes *Essay Concerning Human Understanding*. Start of empiricism. |
| 1710 | Berkeley publishes *Principles of Human Knowledge*, advancing empiricism to new extremes. |
| 1716 | Death of Leibniz. |
| 1739–1740 | Hume publishes *Treatise of Human Nature*, taking empiricism to its logical limits. |
| 1781 | Kant, awakened from his "dogmatic slumbers" by Hume, publishes *Critique of Pure Reason*. |

|       | Great era of German metaphysics begins. |
|-------|------------------------------------------|
| 1807  | Hegel publishes *The Phenomenology of Mind*, high point of German metaphysics. |
| 1818  | Schopenhauer publishes *The World as Will and Representation*, introducing Indian philosophy into German metaphysics. |
| 1889  | Nietzsche, having declared "God is dead," succumbs to madness in Turin. |
| 1921  | Wittgenstein publishes *Tractatus Logico-Philosophicus*, claiming the "final solution" to the problems of philosophy. |
| 1920s | Vienna Circle propounds Logical Positivism. |
| 1927  | Heidegger publishes *Being and Time*, heralding split between analytical and Continental philosophy. |
| 1943  | Sartre publishes *Being and Nothingness*, advancing |

Heidegger's thought and instigating existentialism.

1953    Posthumous publication of Wittgenstein's *Philosophical Investigations*. High era of linguistic analysis.

# Chronology of Aristotle's Life

| | |
|---|---|
| 384 B.C. | Aristotle born at Stagira on the Halkidiki peninsula in northern Greece. |
| 367 B.C. | Enters Plato's Academy in Athens, where he remains for twenty years. |
| 347 B.C. | Leaves Athens after not being appointed head of the Academy on the death of Plato, and takes up residence at the court of Hermias of Atarneus in Asia Minor. |
| 347 B.C. | Marries Pythias. |
| 344 B.C. | Leaves for nearby island of |

|  | Lesbos, where he settles at Mytilene. |
|---|---|
| 343 B.C. | Becomes tutor to the young Alexander the Great. |
| 339 B.C. | Retires to Stagira. |
| 335 B.C. | Returns to Athens and founds the Lyceum as a rival to the Academy. |
| 323 B.C. | Anti-Macedonian feeling in Athens on the death of Alexander causes Aristotle to flee. He takes up residence at Chalkis on the island of Euboea. |
| 322 B.C. | Dies on Euboea, aged sixty-three. |

# Chronology of Aristotle's Era

390 B.C.          Defeat of Rome by the Gauls
                  halts Roman expansion.

380 B.C.          Death of comic playwright
                  Aristophanes.

367 B.C.          Rule by consulship established in
                  Rome. Death of Dionysius I,
                  tyrant of Syracuse, and
                  subsequent brief return of Plato
                  to Sicily.

361–360 B.C.      Plato's third trip to Sicily.

353 B.C.          Death of King Mausolus, who is
                  buried in the Mausoleum, one of
                  the Seven Wonders of the ancient
                  world.

| | |
|---|---|
| 348 B.C. | Second treaty between Rome and Carthage. |
| 347 B.C. | Death of Plato. |
| 335 B.C. | Alexander the Great succeeds his father, Philip II, and sets out on his career of conquest. |
| 326 B.C. | Alexander the Great reaches the gateway to India, his empire stretching at its farthest limit from the Adriatic to beyond the Indus. |
| 323 B.C. | Death of Alexander the Great and ensuing breakup of his empire. |

# Recommended Reading

Jonathan Barnes, ed., *The Cambridge Campanion to Aristotle* (Cambridge University Press, 1993)

John M. Cooper, *Reason and Human Good in Aristotle* (Hackett, 1986)

Abraham Edel, *Aristotle and His Philosophy* (1981)

Martha C. Nussbaum and Amelie O. Rorty, eds., *Essays on Aristotle's De Anima* (Oxford University Press, 1992)

*The Works of Aristotle*, 2 vols. (Encyclopedia Britannica, 1990)

# Index

## A NOTE ON THE AUTHOR

Paul Strathern has lectured in philosophy and mathematics and now lives and writes in London. A Somerset Maugham prize winner, he is also the author of books on history and travel as well as five novels. His articles have appeared in a great many publications, including the *Observer* (London) and the *Irish Times*. His own degree in philosophy was earned at Trinity College, Dublin.